KIDS FUNNIEST KNOCK-KNOCKS

Charles Keller

Illustrated by Jeff Sinclair

Sterling Publishing Co., Inc.

New York

To Gabriel and Bowen

I would like to acknowledge the help of Marcus
Bocchino, Rhoda Crispell, and Brenda Gordon.

Library of Congress Cataloging-in-Publication Available

First paperback edition published in 2001 by
by Sterling Publishing Company, Inc.
387 Park Avenue South, New York, N.Y. 10016
© 2000 by Charles Keller
Distributed in Canada by Sterling Publishing
C/o Canadian Manda Group, One Atlantic Avenue, Suite 105
Toronto, Ontario, Canada M6K 3E7
Distributed in Great Britain and Europe by Chris Lloyd at
Orca Book Services, Stanley House, Fleets Lane,
Poole BH15 3AJ, England.
Distributed in Australia by Capricorn Link (Australia) Pty Ltd.
P.O.Box 704, Windsor, NSW 2756 Australia

Sterling ISBN   0-8069-5920-7 Trade
                0-8069-5882-0 Paper

Knock-Knock.
Who's there?
Abby.
Abby who?
Abby there as soon
as I can.

Knock-Knock.
Who's there?
Abner.
Abner who?
Abner cadabra!

Knock-Knock.
Who's there?
Acoustics.
Acoustics who?
Acoustics help you when you shoot pool.

Knock-Knock.
   Who's there?
Alida.
   Alida who?
Alida of the pack.

   Knock-Knock.
      Who's there?
   Alistair.
      Alistair who?
   Alistair at the TV until I fall asleep.

         Knock-Knock.
            Who's there?
         Allen.
            Allen who?
         Allen a day's work.

Knock-Knock.
  Who's there?
Alpha.
  Alpha who?
Alpha one and one for all.

Knock-Knock.
  Who's there?
Aloha.
  Aloha who?
Aloha myself down the chimney.

Knock-Knock.
  Who's there?
Amanita.
  Amanita who?
Amanita person than you are.

Knock-Knock.
 Who's there?
Ammo.
 Ammo who?
Ammo person who just likes
to knock on doors.

Knock-Knock.
 Who's there?
Amusing.
 Amusing who?
Amusing the phone right now.
 Knock-Knock.
  Who's there?
 Column.
  Column who?
 Column back on the cell phone.

Knock-Knock.
  Who's there?
Argo.
  Argo who?
Argo for broke.

  Knock-Knock.
    Who's there?
  Arlette.
    Arlette who?
  Arlette the cat out of the bag.

  Knock-Knock.
    Who's there?
  Avery.
    Avery who?
  Avery man for himself.

B

Knock-Knock.
Who's there?
Bacchus.
Bacchus who?
Bacchus up against the wall.

Knock-Knock.
Who's there?
Balls.
Balls who?
Balls fair in love and war.

Knock-Knock.
  Who's there?
Barber.
  Barber who?
Barber, black sheep.

Knock-Knock.
  Who's there?
Basis.
  Basis who?
Basis loaded, nobody out!

Knock-Knock.
  Who's there?
Bayou.
  Bayou who?
Bayou self tonight?

Knock-Knock.
 Who's there?
Beacon.
 Beacon who?
Beacon and eggs.

Knock-Knock.
 Who's there?
Beagles.
 Beagles who?
Beagles with cream
cheese.

Knock-Knock.
 Who's there?
Bean.
 Bean who?
Bean there, done that.

Knock-Knock.
 Who's there?
Begonia.
 Begonia who?
Begonia, you're getting
on my nerves!

Knock-Knock.
 Who's there?
Belinda.
 Belinda who?
Belinda or not, I've
come to visit.

Knock-Knock.
     Who's there?
  Bilge.
     Bilge who?
     Bilge a better mousetrap.

Knock-Knock.
  Who's there?
Bin.
  Bin who?
Bin nice knowing you.

Knock-Knock.
  Who's there?
Bitter.
  Bitter who?
Bitter watch your step.

Knock-Knock.
  Who's there?
Blast.
  Blast who?
Blast chance!

Knock-Knock.
  Who's there?
Boise.
  Boise who?
Boise a sore loser!

Knock-Knock.
Who's there?
Bustle.
Bustle who?
Bustle be here in a minute.

Knock-Knock.
Who's there?
Butcher.
Butcher who?
Butcher money where your mouth is.

Knock-Knock.
Who's there?
Byron.
Byron who?
Byron, get one free.

Knock-Knock.
   Who's there?
Candy.
   Candy who?
Candy knock-knock jokes stop now?

Knock-Knock.
   Who's there?
Canoe.
   Canoe who?
Canoe ever forgive me?

Knock-Knock.
  Who's there?
Carey.
  Carey who?
Carey on!

Knock-Knock.
  Who's there?
Carlos.
  Carlos who?
Carlos its fender.

Knock-Knock.
  Who's there?
Casablanca.
  Casablanca who?
Casablanca check.

Knock-Knock.
  Who's there?
Castor.
  Castor who?
Castor pearls before
swine.

OOHH... I NEVER SAUSAGE NICE PEARLS BEFORE!

Knock-Knock.
Who's there?
Census.
Census who?
Census the weekend, we don't have any homework.

Knock-Knock.
Who's there?
Chaos.
Chaos who?
Chaos the letter that comes after J.

Knock-Knock.
Who's there?
Cheese.
Cheese who?
Cheese no spring
chicken.

Knock-Knock.
Who's there?
Chekhov.
Chekhov who?
Chekhov the right box
on the form.

Knock-Knock.
Who's there?
Chester.
Chester who?
Chester country boy.

Knock-Knock.
    Who's there?
Clarify.
    Clarify who?
Clarify come in?

Knock-Knock.
    Who's there?
Clark Kent.
    Clark Kent who?
Clark Kent come, he's sick.

Knock-Knock.
   Who's there?
Coburn.
   Coburn who?
Coburn your clothes.

Knock-Knock.
   Who's there?
Cohen.
   Cohen who?
Cohen around in circles!

Knock-Knock.
   Who's there?
Conan.
   Conan who?
Conan in like
gangbusters.

Knock-Knock.
   Who's there?
Common.
   Common who?
Common up for air.

Knock-Knock.
   Who's there?
Concho.
   Concho who?
Concho be quiet
for a change?

Knock-Knock.
  Who's there?
Congo.
  Congo who?
Congo on like this!

Knock-Knock.
  Who's there?
Corsican.
  Corsican who?
Corsican break down the door...

          Knock-Knock.
            Who's there?
          Cotton.
            Cotton who?
          Cotton trouble again!
                Knock-Knock.
                  Who's there?
                Cosmo.
                  Cosmo who?
                Cosmo trouble than you're worth.

                Knock-Knock.
                  Who's there?
                Crater.
                  Crater who?
                Crater love has no man.

Knock-Knock.
   Who's there?
Cruise.
   Cruise who?
"Cruise afraid of the Big Bad Wolf?"

Knock-Knock.
   Who's there?
Cummings.
   Cummings who?
Cummings in on a wing and a prayer.

Knock-Knock.
  Who's there?
Dachshund.
  Dachshund who?
Dachshund, chicks, and geese flock together.
    Knock-Knock.
      Who's there?
    Debark.
      Debark who?
    Debark is worse than de bite.

Knock-Knock.
  Who's there?
Danielle.
  Danielle who?
Danielle, they can hear you down the block!

      Knock-Knock.
        Who's there?
      De facto.
        De facto who?
      De facto the matter is
      I don't remember my name...

      Knock-Knock.
        Who's there?
      De-icer.
        De-icer who?
      De-icer bigger than de stomach.

Knock-Knock.
  Who's there?
Delores.   Knock-Knock.
  Delores who?   Who's there?
Delores on our side.   Deluxe.
                              Deluxe who?
                            Deluxe of the Irish.

Knock-Knock.
  Who's there?
Dent.
  Dent who?
Dent put the cart before the horse.

Knock-Knock.
  Who's there?
Derive.
  Derive who?
Derive faster, they're gaining on us.

Knock-Knock.
  Who's there?
Detail.
  Detail who?
Detail is wagging the dog.

Knock-Knock.
    Who's there?
Dewey.
    Dewey who?
Dewey have to go to school today?

Knock-Knock.
    Who's there?
Digital.
    Digital who?
Digital anyone I was coming?

Knock-Knock.
    Who's there?
Dispense.
    Dispense who?
Dispense are too tight.

Knock-Knock.
   Who's there?
Ditzy.
   Ditzy who?
"Ditzy small world after all."

Knock-Knock.
   Who's there?
Divest.
   Divest who?
Divest is yet to come.

Knock-Knock.
   Who's there?
Doors.
   Doors who?
Doors not to reason why.

Knock-Knock.
   Who's there?
Droll.
   Droll who?
Droll with the punches.

Knock-Knock.
    Who's there?
Dublin.
    Dublin who?
Dublin over in pain
from all these knock-knock jokes.

Knock-Knock.
    Who's there?
Dune.
    Dune who?
Dune anything tonight?

Knock-Knock.
    Who's there?
Duo.
    Duo who?
Duo die.

Knock-Knock.
    Who's there?
Dwight.
    Dwight who?
Dwight you are
if you think you are!

E

Knock-Knock.
  Who's there?
Earle.
  Earle who?
"Earle be home for
Christmas…"

Knock-Knock.
  Who's there?
Ears.
  Ears who?
Ears looking at you, kid!

FASCINATING!

Knock-Knock.
  Who's there?
Ease.
  Ease who?
Ease up to his old tricks.

Knock-Knock.
  Who's there?
Eaton.
  Eaton who?
Eaton your heart out,
aren't you?

Knock-Knock.
  Who's there?
Eclipse.
  Eclipse who?
Eclipse coupons.

Knock-Knock.
    Who's there?
Eden.
    Eden who?
Eden out of my hand.

Knock-Knock.
    Who's there?
Effie.
    Effie who?
Effie can't say anything nice,
don't say anything at all.

Knock-Knock.
  Who's there?
Eiffel.
  Eiffel who?
Eiffel for it hook, line, and sinker.

Knock-Knock.
  Who's there?
Effigy.
  Effigy who?
Effigy-h-i-j-k.

Knock-Knock.
  Who's there?
Emmon.
  Emmon who?
Emmon your side.

Knock-Knock.
  Who's there?
Endicott.
  Endicott who?
Endicott is where I sleep.

Knock-Knock.
  Who's there?
Ernie.
  Ernie who?
Ernie high to a grasshopper.
  Knock-Knock.
    Who's there?
  Evans.
    Evans who?
  Evans to Betsy!

Knock-Knock.
    Who's there?
Esau.
    Esau who?
Esau the salad dressing.

Knock-Knock.
    Who's there?
Eskimo.
    Eskimo who?
Eskimo questions than I can answer.

Knock-Knock.
Who's there.
Esteban.
   Esteban who?
Esteban the gas, I'm in a hurry.

Knock-Knock.
   Who's there?
Eudora.
   Eudora who?
Eudora doesn't have a bell, so I knocked.

      Knock-Knock.
         Who's there?
      Everett.
         Everett who?
      Everett in this restaurant before?

Knock-Knock.
 Who's there?
Fashion.
 Fashion who?
Fashion your seat belts,
it's going to be a rough ride.

Knock-Knock.
 Who's there?
Faucet.
 Faucet who?
Faucet open if you don't answer the door!

Knock-Knock.
 Who's there?
Fay Row.
 Fay Row who?
Fay Row, the ruler of Egypt!

Knock-Knock.
 Who's there?
Few.
 Few who?
Few only knew what I know, you'd open the door!

Knock-Knock.
Who's there?
Fez.
Fez who?
I say—that's who!

Knock-Knock.
Who's there?
Fiddle.
Fiddle who?
Fiddle bird told me…

Knock-Knock.
Who's there?
Fino.
Fino who?
Fino good reason I knocked on your door.

Knock-Knock.
Who's there?
Five.
Five who?
Five been a pest,
I'm sorry.

Knock-Knock.
Who's there?
Floral.
Floral who?
"Floral Lang Syne."

Knock-Knock.
Who's there?
Foyer.
Foyer who?
Foyer information, it's the Big Bad Wolf.

I'LL HUFF AND I'LL PUFF...
BUT FIRST, I'LL HAVE TO
CALL MY BROKER!

STOCK MARKET

Knock-Knock.
  Who's there?
France.
  France who?
France in need are France indeed.

Knock-Knock.
  Who's there?
Furs.
  Furs who?
Furs come, furs served.

Knock-Knock.
  Who's there?
Gargoyle.
  Gargoyle who?
Gargoyle with a mouthwash every day.

Knock-Knock.
  Who's there?
George Washington.
  George Washington who?
George Washington of dishes.

Knock-Knock.
  Who's there?
Gibbon.
  Gibbon who?
Gibbon the old heave ho!

Knock-Knock.
  Who's there?
Giraffe.
  Giraffe who?
Giraffe tipped over and sank in the lake.

Knock-Knock.
  Who's there?
Glisten.
  Glisten who?
"Glisten my children and you shall hear
of the midnight ride of Paul Revere..."

    Knock-Knock.
      Who's there?
    Gnome.
      Gnome who?
    Gnome is where the heart is.

Knock-Knock.
    Who's there?
Goat.
    Goat who?
Goat up on the wrong side of the bed.

Knock-Knock.
    Who's there?
Godiva.
    Godiva who?
Godiva in the lake!

Knock-Knock.
    Who's there?
Gosset.
    Gosset who?
Gosset down, you're
rocking the boat.

Knock-Knock.
   Who's there?
Gotham.
   Gotham who?
Gotham where I want him.

Knock-Knock.
   Who's there?
Groom.
   Groom who?
Groom service!

Knock-Knock.
   Who's there?
Guyana.
   Guyana who?
Guyana big ego trip.

Knock-Knock.
   Who's there?
Gwen.
   Gwen who?
Gwen it rains, it pours.

H

Knock-Knock.
  Who's there?
Habit.
  Habit who?
Habit off more than I can chew.

Knock-Knock.
  Who's there?
Hallways.
  Hallways who?
Hallways a bridesmaid, never the bride.

Knock-Knock.
  Who's there?
Harmony.
  Harmony who?
Harmony people have knocked on this door?

Knock-Knock.
  Who's there?
Harold.
  Harold who?
Harold do you think I am?

Knock-Knock.
  Who's there?
Heaven.
  Heaven who?
Heaven the time of my life!

Knock-Knock.
  Who's there?
Hedda.
  Hedda who?
Hedda enough of these knock-knock jokes?

Knock-Knock.
  Who's there?
Hewlett.
  Hewlett who?
Hewlett you out of the zoo?

Knock-Knock.
  Who's there?
High Lava.
  High Lava who?
"High Lava parade!"

Knock-Knock.
  Who's there?
Hiram.
  Hiram who?
Hiram at your beck and call.

Knock-Knock.
  Who's there?
Hobby.
  Hobby who?
Hobby go lucky.

Knock-Knock.
  Who's there?
Hoboken.
  Hoboken who?
Hoboken bell, I'll get it fixed.

Knock-Knock.
  Who's there?
Howl.
  Howl who?
Howl you get your pie if you don't open the door?

Knock-Knock.
  Who's there?
Hoyle.
    Hoyle who?
Hoyle never do it again!

Knock-Knock.
  Who's there?
Huguenot.
    Huguenot who?
Huguenot going to believe this...

Knock-Knock.
  Who's there?
Hummus.
  Hummus who?
"Hummus remember this,
a kiss is still a kiss..."

Knock-Knock.
  Who's there?
Ice Cream.
    Ice Cream who?
Ice Cream for you
to open the door!

Knock-Knock.
  Who's there?
Ice Tray.
    Ice Tray who?
Ice Tray off your doorstep, but I'll come back.

Knock-Knock.
   Who's there?
Icon.
   Icon who?
"Icon see clearly now the rain is gone…"

Knock-Knock.
   Who's there?
Ida.
   Ida who?
Ida know, do you?

         Knock-Knock.
            Who's there?
         Iguana.
            Iguana who?
         Iguana go home.

Knock-Knock.
   Who's there?
IHOP.
   IHOP who?
IHOP you have a happy
birthday.

Knock-Knock.
   Who's there?
Ima.
   Ima who?
Ima wild and crazy guy!

Knock-Knock.
   Who's there?
Incas.
   Incas who?
Incas aweigh!

Knock-Knock.
 Who's there?
Industry.
 Industry who?
Industry is where the
bird lives.

Knock-Knock.
   Who's there?
Indy.
   Indy who?
Indy end, you're
going to open the door.

Knock-Knock.
 Who's there?
Injure.
 Injure who?
Injure dreams, wise guy.

Knock-Knock.
   Who's there?
Iota.
   Iota who?
Iota go knock on some
other door.

Knock-Knock.
  Who's there?
Isaac.
  Isaac who?
Isaac as a dog.

      Knock-Knock.
        Who's there?
      Ivory.
        Ivory who?
      Ivory dog has his day.

Knock-Knock.
  Who's there?
Issue.
  Issue who?
Issue the lady of the house?

J

Knock-Knock.
  Who's there?
Jackal.
  Jackal who?
Jackal jump over the candlestick.

Knock-Knock.
   Who's there?
Jake.
   Jake who?
Jake a load off your feet.

Knock-Knock.
   Who's there?
Jamaica.
   Jamaica who?
Jamaica fool of yourself again?

Knock-Knock.
   Who's there?
Jason.
   Jason who?
"Jason the blues away…"

Knock-Knock.
   Who's there?
Jaundice.
   Jaundice who?
Jaundice new soccer club last week.

Knock-Knock.
   Who's there?
Jess.
   Jess who?
Jess or no, are you going to open the door?

Knock-Knock.
   Who's there?
Jester.
   Jester who?
Jester old friend coming to call.

Knock-Knock.
   Who's there?
Jet.
   Jet who?
"Jet a long, little doggie…"

Knock-Knock.
   Who's there?
Jimmy.
   Jimmy who?
Jimmy a break!"

Knock-Knock.
   Who's there?
Joel.
   Joel who?
"Joel Man River…"

Knock-Knock.
   Who's there?
Juan.
   Juan who?
Juan in a million.

Knock-Knock.
Who's there?
Juncture.
Juncture who?
Juncture old car and bought a new one.

Knock-Knock.
Who's there?
Juno.
Juno who?
Juno the ropes?

Knock-Knock.
Who's there?
Justice.
Justice who?
Justice once, try to be nice.

Knock-Knock.
Who's there?
Justin.
Justin who?
Justin the nick of time.

K

OOHHMMMM!!

Knock-Knock.
  Who's there?
Karma.
  Karma who?
Karma before the storm.

Knock-Knock.
  Who's there?
Kelp.
  Kelp who?
Kelp yourself.

Knock-Knock.
  Who's there?
Ken Beebe.
  Ken Beebe who?
Ken Beebe friends?

Knock-Knock.
  Who's there?
Kendall.
  Kendall who?
"Kendall in the wind."

Knock-Knock.
  Who's there?
Kenya.
  Kenya who?
Kenya be quiet over there?
I'm trying to sleep.

Knock-Knock.
  Who's there?
Kenneth.
  Kenneth who?
Kenneth really be
dinner time?

Knock-Knock.
  Who's there?
Kip.
  Kip who?
Kip your shirt on!

Knock-Knock.
  Who's there?
Kipper.
  Kipper who?
Kipper your mouth shut
and your eyes open.

Knock-Knock.
  Who's there?
Kitten.
  Kitten who?
Kitten caboodle.

Knock-Knock.
  Who's there?
Klaus.
  Klaus who?
Klaus the window and
open the door.

Knock-Knock.
  Who's there?
Knotting.
  Knotting who?
Knotting ventured,
knotting gained.

Knock-Knock.
  Who's there?
Kyle.
  Kyle who?
Kyle wait for you outside.

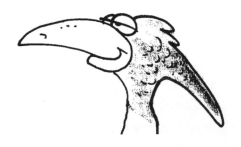

Knock-Knock.
  Who's there?
Lass.
  Lass who?
Lass one out
is a rotten egg.

Knock-Knock.
  Who's there?
Lattice.
  Lattice who?
Lattice and tomato
sandwich.

Knock-Knock.
  Who's there?
Launch.
  Launch who?
Launch is served.

Knock-Knock.
 Who's there?
Lavender.
 Lavender who?
Lavender world laughs with you.

   Knock-Knock.
    Who's there?
   Lecture.
    Lecture who?
   Lecture self go.

      Knock-Knock.
       Who's there?
      Lydia.
       Lydia who?
      Lydia it all hang out.

Knock-Knock.
 Who's there?
Leif.
 Leif who?
Leif me out of it.

      Knock-Knock.
       Who's there?
      Leonie.
       Leonie who?
      Leonie reason I knocked
      is that I forgot my key.

Knock-Knock.
  Who's there?
Leslie.
  Leslie who?
Leslie know, Leslie
forget.

Knock-Knock.
  Who's there?
Lexus.
  Lexus who?
Lexus get this show on
the road.

Knock-Knock.
  Who's there?
Lightning.
  Lightning who?
Lightning your hair, my dear?

Knock-Knock.
  Who's there?
Lisa.
  Lisa who?
Lisa two evils.

Knock-Knock.
  Who's there?
Lois.
  Lois who?
Lois common
denominator.

Knock-Knock.
  Who's there?
Loehmann.
  Loehmann who?
Loehmann on the totem pole.

Knock-Knock.
  Who's there?
Lovitt.
  Lovitt who?
Lovitt or leave it.

Knock-Knock.
  Who's there?
Lucille.
  Lucille who?
Lucille the letter
with a kiss.

Knock-Knock.
  Who's there?
Luke.
  Luke who?
Luke out for number 1.

Knock-Knock.
  Who's there?
Lucas.
  Lucas who?
Lucas up when you get
a chance.

Knock-Knock.
  Who's there?
Lucy.
  Lucy who?
Lucy what I see?

Knock-Knock.
  Who's there?
Lux.
  Lux who?
Lux aren't
everything.

M

Knock-Knock.
   Who's there?
Macon.
   Macon who?
Macon a mountain out of a molehill.

Knock-Knock.
   Who's there?
Madam.
   Madam who?
Madam and Eve.

Knock-Knock.
   Who's there?
Madeira.
   Madeira who?
Madeira, you are
in my power.

Knock-Knock.
  Who's there?
Maia.
  Maia who?
Maia big for your age.

Knock-Knock.
  Who's there?
Marcello.
  Marcello who?
Marcello is out of tune.

Knock-Knock.
  Who's there?
Marissa.
  Marissa who?
Marissa sore from
knocking on your door.

Knock-Knock.
  Who's there?
Megan.
  Megan who?
Megan a fool of yourself as usual.

Knock-Knock.
   Who's there?
Metuchen.
   Metuchen who?
Metuchen you?

Knock-Knock.
   Who's there?
Midas.
   Midas who?
Midas well open up.

Knock-Knock.
   Who's there?
Mezzo.
   Mezzo who?
Mezzo many people I
can't remember my own
name.

Knock-Knock.
   Who's there?
Mischa.
   Mischa who?
Mischa since you've
been away.

Knock-Knock.
   Who's there?
Myer.
   Myer who?
Myer in a bad mood today!
      Knock-Knock.
         Who's there?
      Moose.
         Moose who?
      Moose have been something I ate.

Knock-Knock.
  Who's there?
Nantucket.
  Nantucket who?
Nantucket and
won't give it back.

Knock-Knock.
  Who's there?
Natchez.
  Natchez who?
Natchez another
pretty face.

Knock-Knock.
  Who's there?
Needle.
  Needle who?
Needle the help I can get.

YOU JUST CAN'T KNOCK THIS BOOK!

Knock-Knock.
 Who's there?
Nicole.
 Nicole who?
Nicole out here in the snow!

  Knock-Knock.
   Who's there?
  Nippon.
    Nippon who?
  Nippon tuck.

Knock-Knock.
 Who's there?
Nitwit.
 Nitwit who?
Nitwit me you don't.

  Knock-Knock.
   Who's there?
  Nuance.
    Nuance who?
  Nuance and uncles.

Knock-Knock.
 Who's there?
Norton.
 Norton who?
Norton to write
home about.

Knock-Knock.
  Who's there?
Oblong.
  Oblong who?
Oblong has this been going on?
    Knock-Knock.
      Who's there?
    Ninevah.
      Ninevah who?
    Ninevah business.

Knock-Knock.
   Who's there?
Ocelot.
   Ocelot who?
Ocelot of work you have to do.

      Knock-Knock.
         Who's there?
      Oliver.
         Oliver who?
      Oliver with all my heart.

Knock-Knock.   Knock-Knock.
   Who's there?   Who's there?
Omar.   Ophelia.
   Omar who?   Ophelia who?
"Omar darling,   Ophelia muscle!
Clementine…"

Knock-Knock.
   Who's there?
Oprah.
   Oprah who?
"Oprah the river and through the woods…"

Knock-Knock.
  Who's there?
Orlando.
  Orlando who?
"Orlando the free and the home of the brave."

Knock-Knock.
  Who's there?
Orphan.
  Orphan who?
Orphan running!

Knock-Knock.
  Who's there?
Osage.
  Osage who?
"Osage can you see…"

Knock-Knock.
  Who's there?
Ostrich.
  Ostrich who?
Ostrich in time saves nine.

Knock-Knock.
  Who's there?
Otter.
  Otter who?
Otter the frying pan and into the fire.

        Knock-Knock.
          Who's there?
        Owlet.
          Owlet who?
        Owlet you go first.

Knock-Knock.
  Who's there?
Oz.
  Oz who?
Oz freezing out here in the pouring rain.

P

Knock-Knock.
  Who's there?
Paola.
  Paola who?
Paola bills.

Knock-Knock.
  Who's there?
Papaya.
  Papaya who?
Papaya the sailor man.

Knock-Knock.
  Who's there?
Passion.
  Passion who?
Passion the buck.

Knock-Knock.
　Who's there?
Pasture.
　Pasture who?
Pasture bedtime, isn't it?

　　Knock-Knock.
　　　Who's there?
　　Koto.
　　　Koto who?
　　Koto your room.

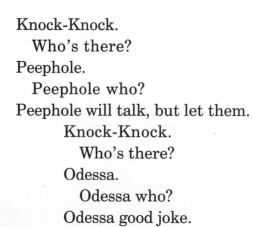

Knock-Knock.
　Who's there?
Peephole.
　Peephole who?
Peephole will talk, but let them.
　　Knock-Knock.
　　　Who's there?
　　Odessa.
　　　Odessa who?
　　Odessa good joke.

Knock-Knock.　　　　Knock-Knock.
　Who's there?　　　　Who's there?
Pious.　　　　　　　Pizza.
　Pious who?　　　　　Pizza who?
Pious in the oven.　　Pizza the action.

Knock-Knock.
  Who's there?
Queasy.
  Queasy who?
Queasy as 1, 2, 3.

OOOHHH...
FIFTY FLIES
are TOO MUCH!

Knock-Knock.
  Who's there?
Quebec.
  Quebec who?
Quebec to the drawing board.

Knock-Knock.
  Who's there?
Quicken.
  Quicken who?
Quicken make beautiful music together.

Knock-Knock.
  Who's there?
Quicksand.
  Quicksand who?
Quicksand for the police!

Knock-Knock.
  Who's there?
Quill.
  Quill who?
Quill wonders never cease!

Knock-Knock.
  Who's there?
Quince.
  Quince who?
Quince some, lose some.

Knock-Knock.
  Who's there?
Quiver.
  Quiver who?
Quiver a big hand.

R

Knock-Knock.
  Who's there?
Rabbit.
  Rabbit who?
Rabbit transit.

Knock-Knock.
  Who's there?
Reston.
  Reston who?
Reston peace.

Knock-Knock.
  Who's there?
Riddle.
  Riddle who?
Riddle things mean a
lot.

Knock-Knock.
　Who's there?
Rita.
　Rita who?
Rita writing on the wall.

Knock-Knock.
　Who's there?
Rolland.
　Rolland who?
Rolland in dough.

Knock-Knock.
　Who's there?
Rook.
　Rook who?
Rook out, the sky is falling!

Knock-Knock.
　Who's there?
Rough.
　Rough who?
Rough, rough, this is your dog speaking.

S

Knock-Knock.
Who's there?
Salada.
Salada who?
Salada nerve asking me
that question.

Knock-Knock.
Who's there?
Señora.
Señora who?
Señora all night and
keep everyone up.

Knock-Knock.
Who's there?
Shutter.
Shutter who?
Shutter up, she's talking too loud.

Knock-Knock.
Who's there?
Siam.
Siam who?
Siam your next door neighbor.

Knock-Knock.
Who's there?
Sinbad.
Sinbad who?
Sinbad and you won't
go to heaven.

Knock-Knock.
Who's there?
Sis.
Sis who?
Sis any way to run
a railroad?

Knock-Knock.
Who's there?
Sonya.
Sonya who?
Sonya wild oats?

Knock-Knock.
Who's there?
Specimen.
Specimen who?
Specimen come to take
you to Mars.

Knock-Knock.
Who's there?
Stairs.
Stairs who?
Stairs no place
like home.

Knock-Knock.
Who's there?
Steak.
Steak who?
Steak it or leave it.

Knock-Knock.
  Who's there?
Stew.
  Stew who?
Stew late to turn
back now.

Knock-Knock.
  Who's there?
Super.
  Super who?
Super salad with
your dinner?

Knock-Knock.
  Who's there?
Surrey.
  Surrey who?
Surrey, wrong door.

Knock-Knock.
  Who's there?
Sven.
  Sven who?
Sven will you ever learn?

Knock-Knock.
  Who's there?
Swatch.
  Swatch who?
Swatch your step!

Knock-Knock.
 Who's there?
Taco.
 Taco who?
Taco my ear off.

Knock-Knock.
 Who's there?
Tacoma.
 Tacoma who?
Tacoma your hair, it's a mess!

Knock-Knock.
 Who's there?
Tattle.
 Tattle who?
Tattle teach you!

Knock-Knock.
  Who's there?
Thaddeus.
  Thaddeus who?
Thaddeus for me to know and you to find out.

Knock-Knock.
  Who's there?
Thermos.
  Thermos who?
Thermos be a doorbell
around here somewhere.

Knock-Knock.
  Who's there?
Thomas.
  Thomas who?
Thomas running out.

Knock-Knock.
  Who's there?
Ticket.
  Ticket who?
Ticket or leave it.

Knock-Knock.
  Who's there?
Topeka.
  Topeka who?
Topeka winner you
have to be lucky.

Knock-Knock.
  Who's there?
Tudor.
  Tudor who?
Tudor victor
belongs the spoils.

Knock-Knock.
  Who's there?
Thoreau.
  Thoreau who?
Thoreau me the ball.

Knock-Knock.
  Who's there?
Tissue.
  Tissue who?
Tissue is too tight.

Knock-Knock.
  Who's there?
Troubadour.
  Troubadour who?
Troubadour is where I
want to go!

Knock-Knock.
  Who's there?
Ubangi.
  Ubangi who?
Ubangi the ceiling,
I'll bang-i the door.

Knock-Knock.
  Who's there?
Udder.
  Udder who?
Udder than that, how did you
like the movie?

Knock-Knock.
  Who's there?
Uniform.
  Uniform who?
Uniform a straight line and stand at attention.

Knock-Knock.
  Who's there?
Unison.
  Unison who?
Unison I never had.

Knock-Knock.
  Who's there?
Usherette.
  Usherette who?
Usherette too much for dinner.

      Knock-Knock.
        Who's there?
      Usury.
        Usury who?
      Usury I come after dinner.

        Knock-Knock.
          Who's there?
        Utica.
          Utica who?
        Utica the words
        right out of my mouth.

V

Knock-Knock.
  Who's there?
Vacancy.
  Vacancy who?
Vacancy from far away
with my binoculars.

Knock-Knock.
  Who's there?
Value.
  Value who?
Value be my
valentine?

Knock-Knock.
  Who's there?
Van.
  Van who?
Van will you ever learn?

Knock-Knock.
  Who's there?
Vanish.
  Vanish who?
Vanish dinner?

Knock-Knock.
  Who's there?
Vaughn.
  Vaughn who?
Vaughn of these days...

Knock-Knock.
  Who's there?
Venom.
  Venom who?
Venom old and gray,
I'll remember this.

Knock-Knock.
　Who's there?
Viaduct.
　Viaduct who?
Viaduct quacks beats me.

Knock-Knock.
　Who's there?
Vilify.
　Vilify who?
Vilify knew my name,
I'd tell you.

Knock-Knock.
　Who's there?
Vino.
　Vino who?
Vino how to make
you talk.

Knock-Knock.
　Who's there?
Violate.
　Violate who?
Violate for school?

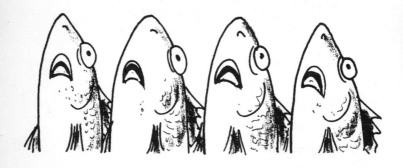

W

Knock-Knock.
  Who's there?
Waddle.
  Waddle who?
Waddle you give me to stop
knocking at your door?

Knock-Knock.
  Who's there?
Wafer.
  Wafer who?
Wafer me.

Knock-Knock.
   Who's there?
Waldo.
   Waldo who?
Waldo wall carpet.

Knock-Knock.
   Who's there?
Weather.
   Weather who?
Weather smoke,
there's fire.

Knock-Knock.
   Who's there?
Wendy.
   Wendy who?
Wendy going gets tough,
the tough get going.

Knock-Knock.
   Who's there?
Wes Q.
   Wes Q. who?
Wes Q. me from these knock-knock jokes!

Knock-Knock.
  Who's there?
Wheelbarrow.
  Wheelbarrow who?
Wheelbarrow your car
and return it tomorrow.

Knock-Knock.
  Who's there?
Whittle.
  Whittle who?
Whittle Orphan Annie.

Knock-Knock.
  Who's there?
Who.
  Who who?
I didn't know you
stuttered.

Knock-Knock.
  Who's there?
Worth.
  Worth who?
Worth cold I ever had.

X

Knock-Knock.
 Who's there?
Xavier.
 Xavier who?
Xavier pennies and the dollars
will take care of themselves.

Knock-Knock.
 Who's there?
Xenia.
 Xenia who?
Xenia someplace before?

GOOD MIRROR!

Knock-Knock.
  Who's there?
Yachts.
  Yachts who?
Yachts new, Pussycat?

Knock-Knock.
  Who's there?
Yeast.
  Yeast who?
Yeast is yeast and west is west.

Knock-Knock.
　Who's there?
Yokum.
　Yokum who?
Yokum up and see me sometime.

Knock-Knock.
　Who's there?
Yucatan.
　Yucatan who?
Yucatan safely if you
wear a sunscreen.

Knock-Knock.
　Who's there?
Yucca.
　Yucca who?
Yucca ask anyone who I
am.

Knock-Knock.
　Who's there?
Yuletide.
　Yuletide who?
Yuletide me over with
a small loan, won't you?

Knock-Knock.
　Who's there?
Yuma.
　Yuma who?
Yuma inspiration!

Knock-Knock.
　Who's there?
Yvonne.
　Yvonne who?
Yvonne to know your
phone number.

Knock-Knock.
  Who's there?
Zagat.
  Zagat who?
Zagat in the Hat.

Knock-Knock.
  Who's there?
Zale.
  Zale who?
Zale ends tomorrow.

Knock-Knock.
Who's there?
Zelda.
Zelda who?
Zelda house.
Knock-Knock.
Who's there?
Zealot.
Zealot who?
Zealot real cheap.

Knock-Knock.
Who's there?
Zeldon.
Zeldon who?
"Zeldon is heard an encouraging word..."

Knock-Knock.
Who's there?
Zen.
Zen who?
Zen what happened?

Knock-Knock.
Who's there?
Zenda.
Zenda who?
Zenda walls came tumbling down.

Knock-Knock.
Who's there?
Zoo.
Zoo who?
Zoo can't win 'em all.

Knock-Knock.
Who's there?
Zys.
Zys who?
Zys is the end!

Knock-Knock.
Who's there?
Zookeeper.
Zookeeper who?
Zookeeper your
shirt on!

Index